To Paul,
Go "Right Down Front"
and enjoy!
Ron Hudson
MJF 9.07

Right Down Front

ron hudson - jazz images

Right Down Front
ron hudson - jazz images

Published by Jazzpress
6816 52nd Avenue South
Seattle, Washington 98118-3469
jazzpress@earthlink.net

In association with
Fish Towne Press
309 Broad Street
Beaufort, North Carolina 28516
marciecarroll@vol.com

Design: Rebecca McMillan
Editorial Direction: Marcie Carroll & Rick Carroll
Foreword: Dr. Herb Wong
Technical Support: Christine Hudson

Cover: Milt Jackson, Modern Jazz Quartet

All images in Right Down Front available as archival prints. Contact jazzpress@earthlink.net or see http://www.ronhudsonjazzphotography.com/

Title inspired by 1960 Sam Jones LP "Right Down Front," reissued as CD 1991, on The Riverside Collection label, featuring Sam Jones, bass and cello; Julian Cannonball Adderley, alto sax; Nat Adderley, cornet; Ron Carter, rhythm bass; Victor Feldman, vibe master; Louis Hayes, drums; Jimmy Heath, arranger and tenor sax. Produced in New York City by Orrin Keepnews.

Portion of proceeds goes to jazz education

ISBN-13 978-0-9796186-0-4
ISBN-10 0-9796186-0-6

Printed in Korea

Library of Congress Cataloging-in-Publication Data
Applied for

For Christine,

My little computer techie—for without you,
there would be no book.

Thank you

Foreword

By Dr. Herb Wong

The history of jazz is documented not only in sound and word, but also in images. Depicting jazz history by photography is a most challenging enterprise, indeed.

Extraordinary jazz photographers have transcended the "stillness" of photographs; namely Herman Leonard, William Gottlieb, Ray Avery, Milt Hinton and David Redfern.

Based on the superb quality of *Right Down Front*, Ron Hudson may well be considered for membership in this coterie of outstanding jazz photographers.

Ron captures legends of jazz and great moments of jazz history in "musically" and visually riveting ways. His images reflect the mosaic of changing moods, colors and humor of jazz in a single palette.

This book is a kind of journey. When you see the images "move" and feel them "moving" they take on a whole different life. The joy of jazz swings and rings with celebration in this serious art form. The annals of jazz are illuminated in Ron's personalized mode of jazz photography.

He selected these images from his quality archive of photos, assembled during more than three decades, with the same degree of discriminating good taste and sensitivity that he applies to his intuitive, meticulous photographic processes.

A book of jazz images expressing historical aspects usually is shaped by the background of the photographer as well as the photograph; in Ron's case, what shines through is his unsparing passion and enthusiasm for the jazz environment—the music, the jazz makers and the jazz venues.

He displays the requisite cumulative jazz literacy, which grew as his interest in certain musicians led him to become increasingly familiar with other artists. Ron's work also reflects his inspirational urge to travel near and far in pursuit of admired performers—from Monterey to Montreux.

Exploring what Ron strives for in his photos gives insight to his pursuits. First, his major objective is getting a portrait. In the majority of images in this book, the musicians are literally alone.

A small handful of the images show two or more artists performing together, and these carry significant meaning; examples include the pairings of Wallace Roney/Wayne Shorter and of bassists Ray Brown/Christian McBride.

Ron is mainly after a portrait of the musicians doing what they do best. Most of them are creating the music while Ron is creating the shot.

Aiming for the optimal artistic shot, he recognizes that some people don't photograph well when they're performing, especially singers who gyrate their jaw to attain tonal eccentricity, plus occasional difficulties with horn players.

Moreover, Ron's code of ethics dictates his unerring good taste. He strives not to put a photo for public consumption that fails to meet his standard of quality, illustrated by his tenacity in finally getting his portrait of guitarist Pat Metheny—after five separate previous opportunities.

At any venue, he refrains from being intrusive and sometimes misses some shots because of it. Also, he experiences a strong emotional rush when he reacts to the performance of certain artists, despite having heard the sounds dozens of times. As he describes, the experience "gets me in the pit of my stomach." Witnessing the Count Basie Band playing Neal Hefti's gorgeous piece "Lil' Darlin," brought Ron to tears.

Other features in the book mirroring Ron's perspectives include subjects that bridge generations of jazz history, from senior jazz rhythm guitarist Danny Barker to precocious teenaged piano genius Eldar Djangirov.

Ron's delightful anecdotes are rewarding historical bites that bring the eye of his camera into engaging interplay. They function as entertaining entre-acts for the book.

Because Ron has a measure of musical background himself, he knows when a pianist is going to come down hard on the keys. He waits for the artist to do it and shoots at that decisive moment.

On the other hand, Ron will shoot an entire roll of film on one artist to get a perfect shot.

Ron was musically nourished from an early age, even as his artistic talents emerged in visual arts. He had an eye, and he had an ear. Later, he was able to merge his interests in his artistic contributions in jazz photography.

When he was a little tyke living in Oakland, California, he went up an escalator with his mother at Capwell's department store around Christmas time. At the top was a full drum set, and it topped his holiday wish list (unrealistic at age 4!). Next, he took up the trumpet in school, but his interest in it faded. He resumed his focus on drums at age 23, taking percussion lessons, and he still plays on occasion.

In addition, he became a studied listener of recordings—a practice that started at age 8, back in the days when his dad, Oliver, ran The Hudson Music Co. in Santa Maria, a business that placed jukeboxes in bars and restaurants. Record labels like Capitol and Columbia kept them supplied with current 78s. Ron was immersed in the sounds of swing, early bebop and blues.

On the radio he heard the big bands and popular band singers—Helen Forrest, Peggy Lee, Jo Stafford, *et al*. As a teenager he began seeing live performances at the Rose Garden Ballroom in Pismo Beach. He was ecstatic when he first heard saxophonist Earl Bostic. He really didn't know who the musician was, but he liked the music and bought Bostic's records. At another concert, he was so turned on by the stellar slate of the Dave Brubeck Quartet, Art Farmer/Benny Golson Jazztet and Maynard Ferguson's Powerhouse 13-piece band that he proclaimed this was going to be the music of his life.

In the meantime, Ron's abilities for creating visual images surfaced and his innate artistic assets were honed in high-school art classes, followed by college-level training in the Air Force, where he served as a broad-scope illustrator. Being in the military allowed him opportunities to travel and enjoy many jazz venues far and wide from wherever he was stationed.

Serendipitously in 1959, he came home on leave to visit his parents, who had moved to the Monterey peninsula.

Ron first attended the Monterey Jazz Festival in its second year. He became a rabid fan and attended the MJF off and on as a devotee—until 1973, when he was first credentialed as a photographer from Hawai'i, where he lived from 1970 until he relocated to Seattle in 1992.

As his booklist of photos indicates, Ron has covered his major source venue—the MJF—every year between 1974 and 2006, among other venues.

Yours truly has attended the MJF as a member of the jazz press since its birth in 1958, and I've rubbed elbows with Ron for nearly three decades, after first meeting him at the 1978 Russian River JazzFest when I was its Artistic Director.

Like his images, Ron has always reflected kindred ideals of spontaneity, keen insight and human warmth. Cultivating jazz as a way of life, Ron is stimulated by the music. It sustains his work and pleasures with jazz images. He possesses an unwavering commitment to life-long creativity and learning, articulated in the seductive artistry of his jazz images. And his richest gift to us is his ability to transcend the camera itself.

Right Down Front is a perfect thematic concept and title for this book as it literally takes the viewer of these images right down front for an intimate experience in the front row diggin' it right smack in the eye!

Ron Hudson has categorically carved an imagination-filled singular niche in jazz photography that sings and swings.

Dig it: Right Down Front!

Herb Wong

Jazz Historian

Dr. Herb Wong, an internationally respected jazz journalist, historian, critic and concert producer, hosted "Jazz Perspectives" at KJAZ-FM in San Francisco for 35 years.

Past president of International Association for Jazz Education (IAJE), he was inducted into the IAJE Hall of Fame in 1993.

As president and chief producer for Palo Alto and Blackhawk record labels, Dr. Wong has been responsible for more than 130 jazz recordings. He has produced CD-ROM multimedia and interactive titles for eBook, Inc., and Smart CD, Inc.

A noted jazz writer, Dr. Wong has authored program notes for hundreds of jazz recordings and contributed reviews in numerous journals.

He wrote *The Ultimate Jazz Fake Book* (Hal Leonard), which includes 625 standards and jazz classics.

Dr. Wong serves on boards of the Harlem Jazz Hall of Fame, National Big Band and Jazz Hall of Fame, National Academy of Recording Arts and Sciences, and Manhattan Arts-American Music Center.

He has participated on National Endowment for the Arts Music Recording and Jazz Fellowship panels and has served as a technical consultant for Smithsonian Institution's Oral Jazz History Program.

Dr. Wong lectures at Stanford University and has taught at Western Washington University and University of California at Berkeley.

Dr. Wong earned bachelor of arts and doctor of education degrees from University of California at Berkeley and a master of arts degree from San Jose State University.

Jazz—

One soaring moment.

Photography—

A gift of image offered
by one and received by another.

Photographer—

The eye that captures that
translucent exchange of
energy known as art.

—VICTORIA MEDGYESI

Art Farmer

Saturday evening, August 29, 1959, Bushnell Memorial Hall, Hartford, Connecticut. Art Farmer, Benny Golson and the Jazztet. Art's twin brother, Addison, on bass, Curtis Fuller, trombone, and I'm guessing, McCoy Tyner at piano, and maybe Lex Humphries on drums. I'd never been exposed to music like that before. Same night, same show: Dave Brubeck Quartet with Paul Desmond, and Maynard Ferguson's 13-piece band, with singer Anne Marie Moss. What a night! I was 19 years old and I knew I had found the music of my life. And the ticket only cost $3.60.

Monterey Jazz Festival 1986

Benny Golson

The Art Farmer / Benny Golson Jazztet had just finished their set and I was back stage waiting for the big door stage left to swing open after the curtain closed. I was hoping to get some candid shots. The door swung open and there he stood—smiling as if he knew I was coming to take his picture. He doesn't look like a guy who would write a tune and call it "Killer Joe."

Monterey Jazz Festival 1986

Maynard Ferguson

I saw Maynard Ferguson first in 1959, and many times since. He was a favorite at Dimitriou's Jazz Alley, and I'd go hear him every time he came to town. Over the years we had several conversations, mostly about drummers in his many bands. He had a gift for conversation, gave you his undivided attention, made you feel comfortable. He did that with his trumpet, too. I miss his high register, and his Big Bop Nouveau Band.
Tech note: 180mm lens, f5.6 at 60th of a sec.

Dimitriou's Jazz Alley, Seattle 2002

Lalo Schifrin

In the early 60's, I lived in Goose Bay, Labrador, north of St. Johns, Newfoundland, courtesy of Uncle Sam's Air Force. I prayed that some day the Base Exchange would have jazz. Finally, there it was: Lalo Schifrin's "Gillespiana" for $3.65. I couldn't go wrong. It's now framed and hangs proudly in my home, autographed by Dizzy and Lalo. On Friday evening, September 20, 1996, the Carnegie Hall Jazz Band, directed by Jon Faddis, performed "Gillespiana" with special guest Lalo Schifrin. I think Dizzy would have liked the festivities.

Monterey Jazz Festival 1996

Dr. Lonnie Smith

Say "Hammond B3 Organ" to me, and I think of Jimmy Smith, Jack McDuff, Rhona Scott, and Dr. Lonnie Smith. He's been playing the B3 a long, long time with some of the best musicians in jazz. If you like straight-ahead jazz or just down-dirty greasy funk, this is your man.

Tech note: Sitting on the floor with a monopod and a 300mm lens.

International Association for Jazz Education Conference, New York 2006

Cal Tjader

After Air Force boot camp, I visited the Italian side of my family—Aunt Rose and Uncle Beck in San Anselmo, north of San Francisco. "What would you like to do in the City?" Aunt Rose asked. "Top of The Mark for cocktails, Vanessi's for dinner," I said, "and Blackhawk, corner of Turk and Hyde, to hear Cal Tjader."

Monterey Jazz Festival 1981

Poncho Sanchez

One night after his gig a few years ago, I told Poncho Sanchez how good his group sounded and how tastefully he presented all the music. "If there was one thing I learned from my years with Cal Tjader," he said, "it was to be tasteful." He knew I was a big Cal Tjader fan.

Dimitiou's Jazz Alley, Seattle 2001

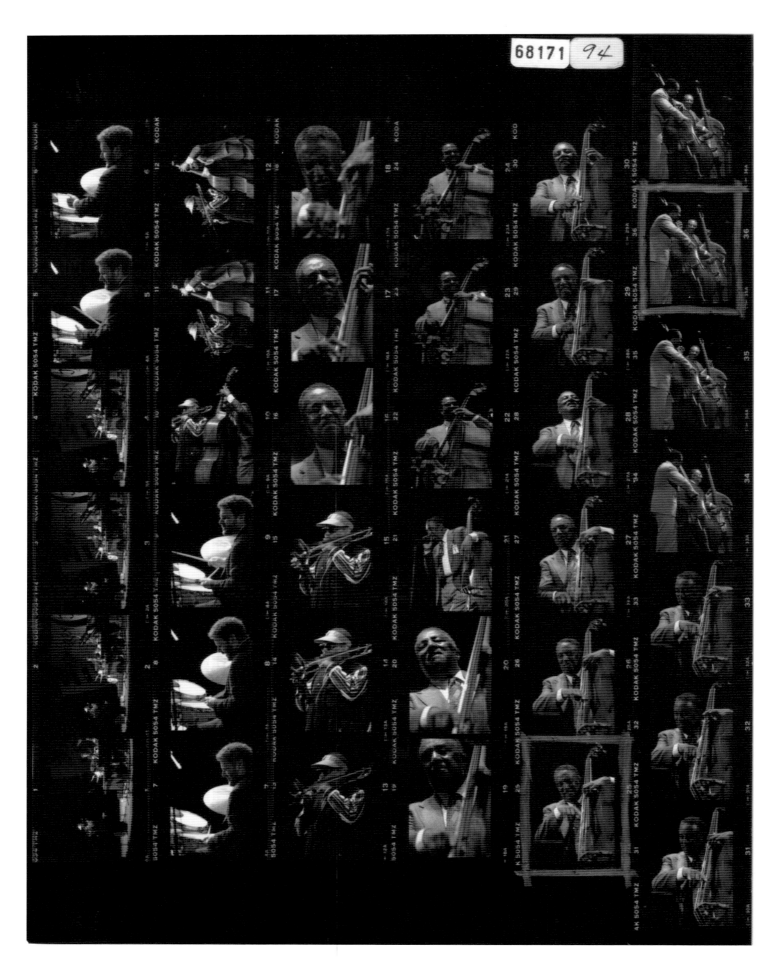

Christian McBride and Ray Brown, Monterey Jazz Festival 1994

Ray Brown
& Christian McBride

What we have here is the torch passing from one generation to the next—
Ray Brown, 68, and Christian McBride, 22, together in what one critic called
"a stunning bass duet." "Thank you for capturing history," McBride told me
later.

Monterey Jazz Festival 1994

Jon Hendricks

Singing masters of ceremony, on closing night at Monterey in 1959, Lambert, Hendricks and Ross opened the show with their own set, then sang introductions for Count Basie, Oscar Peterson and Sarah Vaughan. A few years ago, I talked to Jon Hendricks about that night. "You know," he said, "in between sets, Dave, Annie and I were backstage trying to come up with lyrics for the next introduction. But we made it!"

Monterey Jazz Festival 1996

Ron McCroby

"You know how to whistle, don't you?" Lauren Bacall asked in *To Have and To Have Not*. "Just put your lips together and blow." Well, Ron McCroby sure could blow his "pucculo." Absolutely amazing. He whistled at Monterey in '82, '83, and '87, signed with Concord Jazz, won CLIO Awards, and appeared on the "Tonight Show." He signed this image, "To Ron, What a Jam-Up Photographer." He died in August, 2002.

Monterey Jazz Festival 1983

Toshiko Akiyoshi

The 1976 Monterey Jazz Festival was my first opportunity to photograph Toshiko. Again at the Concord Jazz Festival in '78. By then I'd shot three rolls of film without a good image. In Monterey in 1981, through one of the portholes backstage, there she was with her back to the audience, facing her band between the trumpet section and drummer. She was looking right into my lens, smiling as if to say, "You've waited long enough, here's your shot." I ran a burst of five or six frames before she turned to sit at the piano. I got lucky, again!

Monterey Jazz Festival 1981

Joe Venuti

Born on a boat coming to America from Italy in 1904, Joe Venuti was a classically trained violinist who thought playing jazz was a lot more fun. He sure was. He led me to Stephane Grappelli and Regina Carter. In this shot (note position of bow) he's in the sun, having fun with Woody Herman Orchestra, one year before he died.

Pacific Kool Jazz Fair, Waikiki, Honolulu, Hawai'i 1977

René Marie

After shooting Main Arena artists one night at Monterey, I headed for Dizzy's Den to check out this singer. I came in the back door, said hello to the guard, and asked, "How is she?" "She's great, man, you're gonna love her." When René Marie began to sing "Suzanne" (a Leonard Cohen composition) over the top of "Bolero," I almost fell down. What a concept, so beautifully done. For a lady self-taught, she taught herself well.

Monterey Jazz Festival 2002

Stan Kenton

I got out of a sick bed to photograph Stan Kenton in Hawai'i. I was an upstart jazz photographer, and this was my first opportunity. I loved all that brass and heavy bottomed reed section. I bought every album for 20 years. Sick or not, the show goes on, and the photographer must get his shot.

Tech note: Nikon FTN, 105mm lens, f5.6 at 125th of a second, Kodak Safety Film 400 push to 1600.

Tapa Ballroom, Hilton Hawaiian Village Hotel, Honolulu, Hawai'i 1975

Jean "Toots" Thielemans

I stood in line for an hour and a half to have *Q The Autobiography of Quincy Jones* auto-graphed. During that time I was wondering what I was going to say. I stepped up, shook Quincy's hand, and told him how much I admired how he utilized the harmonica talent of Toots on many of his albums. "Oh, thank you," he said. "Toots is a wonderful talent, and we are good friends; I spoke to him this morning." Give a listen to "Brasil Project" and "Body Heat."

Monterey Jazz Festival 1995

Louis Bellson

The Russian River Jazz Festival is staged outdoors in broad daylight on
a river that runs down to the Pacific. The bandstand appears to float on
the river. Funny place to find Louis Bellson. But there he was, pale faced,
blinking in bright sunshine, so out of his natural element. His performance
in the great outdoors brought down the house. It still makes me smile.

Russian River Jazz Festival 1978

Martin Taylor

I'm not too crazy about solo shows. I like bass and drums. This was not one of those times. A good friend for whom I have a lot of respect as a guitar player said, "Go see Martin Taylor first chance you get, he's a killer." He was right. Taylor's unbelievable, with great stage presence and a wonderful sense of humor. I was totally entertained.

Tech note: Nikon F100, 180mm lens, Kodak TMZ 3200.

Dimitriou's Jazz Alley, Seattle 2004

Ahmad Jamal

Like a lot of other people in 1958, I ran out and bought Ahmad Jamal's "At the Pershing" after hearing his version of "Poinciana." I was living in upstate New York, doing time in an Air Force uniform. Every jukebox in the state of New York featured "Poinciana." I went crazy for the whole album. I played it so much that it turned a light gray and would skip all over the place. I replaced the album twice and then at last got a CD. I still listen to it, and it is in the rotation whenever my wife and I have a dinner party. I finally got to see Ahmad live at Blues Alley in Washington, DC, in the mid-80s. No camera; just enjoyed.

Atlanta Jazz Festival 2004

Richard Bona

I first heard Richard Bona play bass and sing at Monterey in 2000.
The young man from Cameroon has been busy since moving to New York
in 1995. He's been featured in the Joco Pastorius Big Band, and has
worked with The Brecker Brothers, Steve Gadd, Herbie Hancock, Joe
Zawinul, David Sanborn, and Pat Metheny to name a few. I like this
image because the light was just right for a change. He liked it too!

Tech note: Nikon 8008s, 180mm lens, f5.6 at 250th of a second, Kodak TMZ 3200.

Monterey Jazz Festival 2000

Clark Terry

Of all the jazz artists I've photographed, Clark Terry turns out to be the one I photographed most—16 times—so it's difficult to pick one shot. This may be it, the only one with two horns: flugel and trumpet. He took turns on each. What chops! Even now, at 80-something.

Monterey Jazz Festival 1988

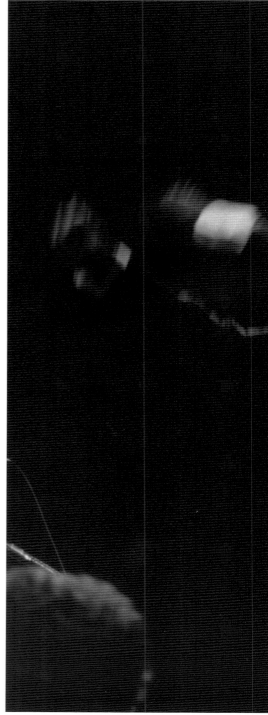

Gerald Wilson

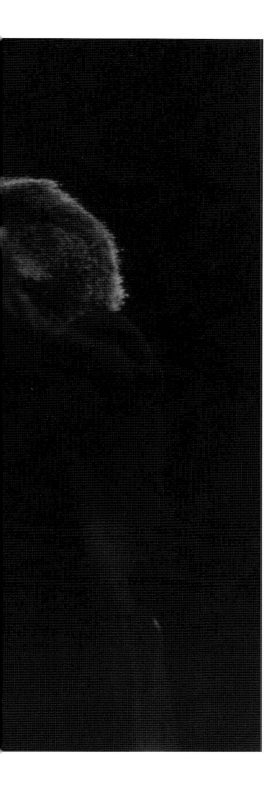

Gerald Wilson

Gerald Wilson pulls notes out of his orchestra. He's great fun to watch but difficult to get right on film.
I always burned a roll or two trying to get a decent shot. Here are three of some 250 exposures taken
over five years of appearances. You don't go out, take a picture of Mr. Wilson, and go home.

Monterey Jazz Festival 1990

Dame Cleo Laine
& Sir John Dankworth

What a great pair they are. Cleo sings; John plays. And can she sing. With her smoky, bold, imaginative voice, she's been nominated for Grammys in Female Jazz, Popular and Classical categories. My first notice of Cleo was "Send in the Clowns," an anthem of hers for years that still grabs me.

Dimitriou's Jazz Alley, Seattle 2005

Matt Wilson

Matt Wilson told me at a clinic to "get to know your drum kit" by eating with it. Breakfast, lunch, dinner, or maybe just a cup of coffee. I'll try anything to play better. One afternoon, ham and cheese in one hand, glass of pale ale in the other, I went to sit down behind my kit, snagged my foot on the snare stand and pale ale, mustard, mayo, ham, cheese, lettuce and whole wheat bread went everywhere. During the hour-long cleanup, we got even better acquainted.

Ballard Jazz Festival, Seattle 2004

Eiji Kitamura

Eiji Kitamura, the "Benny Goodman of Japan," is a fixture at Monterey.
I've photographed him often. When I went to see him at Club Monaco in
Tokyo in 1984, I brought two prints of this shot, one for him, one for me.
He introduced me as the "famous jazz photographer from Monterey."
"I am honored," he said, "you came all this way to see me."

Monterey Jazz Festival 1981

Wynton Marsalis

First saw Wynton in '83 in Hawai'i at the Honolulu Symphony. After the concert, back stage, he received a steady stream of young students who had musical questions. He stayed a good hour and a half with the kids. I was struck by how young he was. Only 22 at the time.

Monterey Jazz Festival 2001

Joe Williams

Think jazz artists aren't fussy about what they wear? I took this picture in 1983. Or so I thought. That's what I wrote on the print. Next time I saw him, I gave him a copy. "I think the date you have here is wrong," he said. "I wasn't wearing that jacket that year."

Monterey Jazz Festival 1983 (or maybe not)

James Moody

When Monterey Jazz Festival's Jimmy Lyons staged "Saturday Night Jive with Dizzy and Friends," Gillespie's good friend James Moody took care of business with his masterpiece, "Moody's Mood for Love." Other friends included Ray Brown, Red Garland, Milt Jackson, Arnett Cobb, and Mickey Roker. It was one sweet evening of jazz.

Monterey Jazz Festival 1978

Ramsey Lewis

I asked Ramsey Lewis to autograph this image for me couple of years ago at Monterey. It's more than 30 years old. "I haven't seen myself that young in a long time," he said. I took him down Memory Lane. "First time I heard you live was at the Colony jazz club down on Alvarado Street right here in Monterey." That was the "In Crowd" days.

Tech note: Kodak Safety Film 400, push to 1600, f5.6 at 60th of a second.

Waikiki Shell, Honolulu, Hawai'i 1974

Sonny Rollins

Sonny never stops moving when he plays. He moves all over the stage. In and out of range. And his horn is always going up and down. A perpetual-motion player. I focus on his nose and let the rest of the shot do what it does. Sometimes it works.

Monterey Jazz Festival 1994

Michael Brecker

Living in Hawai'i was great! But the isolation kept you from knowing what was going on musically. You were busy working, trying to pay the rent, put papaya on the table, and maintain your tan. I heard a jazz group called "Steps Ahead" was in town. That's how I discovered Michael Brecker. The (13) Grammy Award-winning saxophonist died in January, 2007.

Gabe's in Waikiki, Honolulu, Hawai'i 1982

Herbie Mann

The most influential flute player in jazz history set a breathless pace. No. 1 in the *Down Beat* poll for 13 years. Gold records galore. Concerts around the world. He played Latin, Brazilian, disco, even Jewish and Turkish music. With his last note in the air, he points to his piano player: "You take it home, baby—I'm done."

Monterey Jazz Festival 1999

Elvin Jones

'Round midnight backstage after the last set at Seattle's Jazz Alley, hanging out with Elvin Jones. He's in cool-down mode, in a white full-length terry cloth robe. We talk about drums and stuff until his wife, Keiko, all of four-foot-nothing, appears, looks at her watch, and says: "Elvin, it's time for you to go to bed."

Dimitriou's Jazz Alley, Seattle 2001

Dianne Reeves

I love photographing Dianne Reeves. She's so dynamic, so animated and so beautiful when she sings that you can't help but get a good shot.

Monterey Jazz Festival 1993

Dizzy Gillespie

Always full of mischief, Dizzy Gillespie did his best to intimidate this young trumpet player, but the young man kept his cool and went right on playing.

Monterey Jazz Festival 1997

Tito Puente

I cut my Latin teeth at seventeen on Cal Tjader. Tito Puente was next.
I met Tito in the Green Room at Jazz Alley in Seattle. We were talking
percussion." Do you still woodshed?" I asked. "Yes," he said, "I use rebar
to stay in shape." El Rey, forever young.

Tech note: This is the one and only time I used a starburst filter, but it seemed to work.

Monterey Jazz Festival 1993

Gabor Szabo

In the mid-60's I heard Gabor's album "Bacchanal" and liked it even
though it was pop and commercial. His sound was instantly recognizable.
A self-taught guitarist, he worked with drum great Chico Hamilton,
vibist Gary McFarland and Charles Lloyd. He died in 1982, just short
of his 46th birthday.

Tech note: Nikon FTN, 200mm lens, Kodak Safety Film 400 push to 1600.

Waikiki Shell, Honolulu, Hawai'I 1974

Benny Green

He was 14 when I first saw him playing piano with the California High School All-Star Big Band on Sunday afternoon at Monterey. Sixteen years later, Saturday night, Main Stage: Benny Green at the piano, this time with The Ray Brown Trio. Once an all-star, always an all-star.

Monterey Jazz Festival 1994

Paul Desmond

Memorial Day, May 30, 1977, bad news on the radio: "Paul Desmond Dead of Cancer at 52." I had just taken this photograph of him a few months earlier with his group at a jam session. He was the first alto player out of the post-Bop era who didn't sound like Bird. I liked him. To me this is a small piece of jazz history—the last photograph I took of him.

Monterey Jazz Festival 1976

John Clayton

I love to hear John Clayton play his bass. What a beautiful tone it has. I have this curiosity about basses: I like to know how old they are, particularly when they have that old-world patina, like John's. I've asked many a bass player, "How old is your bass?" John holds the record for oldest bass, at least with me. He told me he has documentation dating back 409 years. Imagine the stories it could tell. That's where that beautiful tone comes from—the instrument, and of course, the man who plays it.

Monterey Jazz Festival 2003

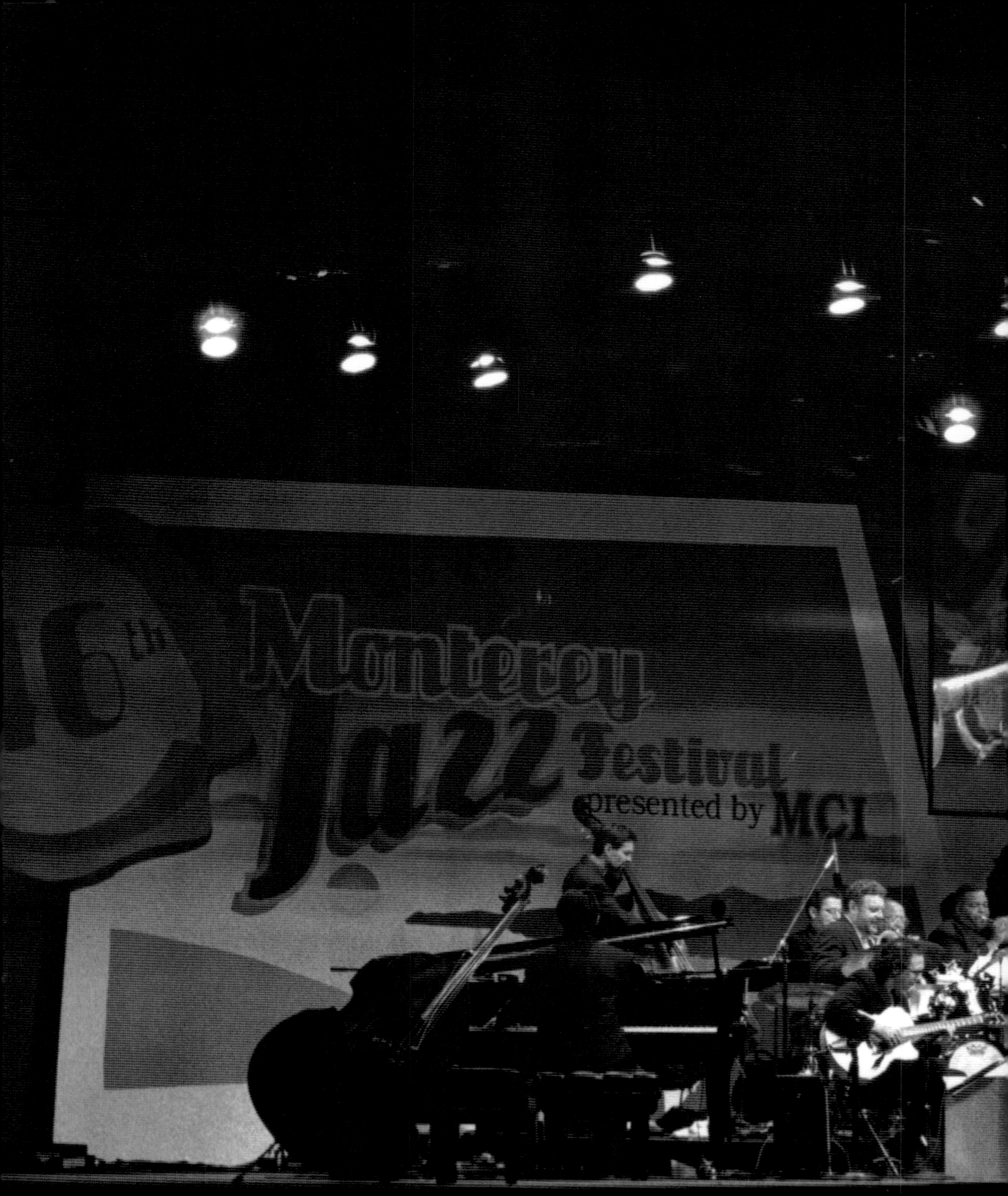
Monterey Jazz Festival
presented by MCI

Clayton /
Hamilton
Jazz
Orchestra

It was getting late, and my
feet hurt. I'd been shooting
since noon. I went to say
hello to my wife, sit down
awhile, enjoy the big band.
But just sitting there, I felt
I should still be shooting.
I grabbed my Nikon F100
camera and 80 mm lens out
of my bag. Got this from my
seat. There's energy in this
photograph. Can you hear
it?

Monterey Jazz Festival 2003

Tierney Sutton

Usually, I watch a performer run through one or two tunes before I lift the camera. This night the stage was down lighted from the side, throwing a cool back light on Tierney Sutton. With my long lens I repositioned myself and tried for the right exposure on her face. I was looking to back light her blonde hair as she sang.

Dimitriou's Jazz Alley, Seattle 2003

Stan Getz

In the cold, frozen tundra of Labrador, back in my Air Force days, I had a stereo with turntable at my office. One Saturday afternoon I went to the Base Exchange to see what was new in the record department. Bingo! Stan Getz' "Jazz Samba." Couldn't get back to my office fast enough. I played it all afternoon. The Bossa Nova had arrived in Goose Bay.

Monterey Jazz Festival 1990

Woody Herman

As a kid in the late 40's and early 50's, I listened to the radio a lot. A local station's afternoon music show used Woody Herman's "Four Brothers" as the theme song. This was Woody's Second Herd that included Zoot Sims, Al Cohn and Stan Getz. "Four Brothers" was a hit and so was my favorite, "Early Autumn." I heard the band live for the first time in 1960, then photographed it in '79, '82, '83, '85, and '87. Woody Herman died October 29, 1987—a month after this shot was taken.

Monterey Jazz Festival 1987

Joe Locke

If you like vibes, you'll like Joe. Bebop, fusion, avant-garde: he pushes the envelope every time. I had his "State of Soul" CD before he hit Seattle for the Ballard Jazz Festival in 2005. His set was recorded—Joe Locke / Geoffrey Keezer Group, "Live in Seattle." His "Rev-elation" is a tribute to our cover artist, Milt Jackson.

Ballard Jazz Festival, Seattle 2005

Stephane Grappelli

There's something about the violin. After hearing Joe Venuti in 1977, I grew fond of jazz violinists. I'm a big fan of Regina Carter and Stephane Grappelli. Some of his licks sound very Old World European to me, like something my Italian grandfather might have played. This tight shot of Grappelli shows his concentration. As I listen and close my eyes, I'm in Paris.

Monterey Jazz Festival 1995

Regina Carter

I deliberately got in the same position with the same camera (Nikon 8008S), same lens, (180 mm) and same film (Kodak 3200 ASA) so someday I could put her next to Stephane Grappelli. It was an indulgence but who could say no to bookend shots? She exhibits serene confidence in this image of a jazz virtuoso of the violin. Carter, you must know, is the only jazz violinist invited to play Paganini's Stradivarius. Imagine Paganini hearing her play "Free Fall" on his violin.

Monterey Jazz Festival 1999

Albert "Tootie" Heath

I never really had an opportunity to interact with Tootie as I did with his brothers, Jimmy and Percy. He is an excellent hard bop player. Debut recording with John Coltrane in 1957. He worked with a variety of groups— Art Farmer and Benny Golson's Jazztet, Dexter Gordon, Wes Montgomery and Herbie Hancock. In 1975, the three brothers formed the Heath Brothers. Tootie left the group after three years to freelance, teach at the Stanford Jazz Workshop and lead a legendary jazz drum ensemble called The Whole Drum Truth.

Monterey Jazz Festival 1993

Tania Maria

Tania Maria, a high-energy Brazilian soaked in samba, was knocking 'em out on this Saturday night in Monterey with "Come With Me." Billed as "Viva Carnaval," the evening included Tito Puente with Cal Tjader and Poncho Sanchez, Flora Purim, Airto Moreira, and Batucaje a Carnaval, a dance and percussion group.

Tech note: Nikon FM2, 200mm lens, f8 at 125th of a second.

Monterey Jazz Festival 1981

Danny Barker

In bowler hat, pin-striped suit, fingers festooned with gold and diamond rings, New Orleans-born Danny Barker looks like he just stepped off a Mardi Gras float. He's playing a Joe Pass signature guitar.

Monterey Jazz Festival 1993

Eldar Djangirov

Early Sunday mornings at Monterey, jazz photographers meet for breakfast.
Gerald Wilson, who often joins us, invited Eldar Djangirov, a young, Russian-
born teenage piano prodigy, and he just happened to sit across from me.
"You're not going to believe how good he is," a colleague said. "He scorches
the keyboard." Eldar's first CD, "Eldar," proves jazz today is alive and well.

Dimitriou's Jazz Alley 2005

Scott Hamilton

This image of Scott Hamilton seems to have a 1940's feel about it. Maybe it's the jacket or his mustache. I can hear his swinging, warm tenor saxophone. Sitting next to him on this gig was Warren Vache, cornet; Cal Collins, guitar; Monty Budwig, bass; and Jake Hanna, drums. A four-star player, Hamilton tours Europe and the US, has 40 albums as a leader, mostly on the Concord label.

Concord Jazz Festival 1978

Butch Miles

The year after I took this photo of Butch, the Basie Band did a one-nighter at the Honolulu Concert Hall. After the show, I had an opportunity to talk to Butch for a few minutes as he was taking down his drum kit. I noticed he was soaking wet with perspiration through his very dapper gray suit. "Butch, you sweat your butt off behind that drum kit," I said. "Yeah, and I sometimes lose five to six pounds every night I play a gig. I just want to go back to the hotel and go to bed." Oh, the life of a big-band drummer. Arguably one of the great big-band drummers of his generation.

Monterey Jazz Festival 1977

Russell Malone

A few years ago at Jazz Alley, Russell Malone was performing with Diana Krall. Halfway through the set some bozo in the audience was talking loud, atypical of Seattle audiences. Russell stared hard at him, then put his finger to his lips, and went, "Shhhhhhh," real loud. The guy shut up. The show went on. Malone can be intimidating on guitar too. Check out his CD, "Sweet Georgia Peach."

Centrum's Jazz Port Townsend 2005

Bud Shank

Bud Shank always greets me, "Hi Bud," and I always say, "Hi Ron." Private joke. A few years ago, the Port Townsend paper ran Bud's photo (above) with a caption that said, "Ron Hudson, alto sax player, appears this week-end." And credited "Photo by Bud Shank."

Centrum's Jazz Port Townsend 2003

Jimmy Scott

I had never seen him on stage before, the man they called "Little Jimmy Scott." Lionel Hampton tagged him with that when he joined the band in 1948. Rediscovered in 1991, he emerged with a Grammy-nominated CD, "All The Way," and now has legions of fans all over the world, including Madonna. "Jimmy Scott is the only singer who can make me cry," she once said. While I was photographing him I had to stop, and listen, and she's right. His ballads are simply the best.

Dimitriou's Jazz Alley, Seattle 1998

David Friesen

On Johnny Carson one night I heard David Friesen say he was most proud of "Children of The Kingdom," a solo bass performance he wrote for Monterey in 1977 to delight—and silence—the rowdy audience. I said, "Hey, I think I've got that shot." I gave it to him and made a friend. In 1994, at Centrum's Jazz Port Townsend I took this shot that shows his intensity. He liked it enough to use for a publicity shot.

Centrum's Jazz Port Townsend 1994

Modern Jazz Quartet

Flash photography is taboo at Monterey. Stage lights drop off fast when you back away. To get this shot I used my 105 mm lens and Ilford 3200 film, shutter wide open at a 1/60th of a second. I cleaned up hot spots later. Some shots are made in heaven, others in the dark room.

Monterey Jazz Festival 1991

The players: (l-r)
John Lewis, piano;
Percy Heath, bass;
Milt Jackson, vibes;
Connie Kay, drums

Oscar Peterson
& Jimmy Lyons

Two old friends on stage before the curtain opened. Don't know what the joke was. Or even if it was a joke. Just a candid moment in the lives of the late Jimmy Lyons, Monterey Jazz Festival founder, and Oscar Peterson.

Monterey Jazz Festival 1990

Michael "Patches" Stewart
& Kenny Garrett

I like that trumpet and sax sound when they play together. It's the sound of jazz. When I look at this image of Michael "Patches" Stewart and Kenny Garrett, I think of the sound of jazz coming at you. Patches' nickname came from high school days when it was cool to wear patches on your jeans. I like to listen to Patches on "Blue Patches" and Kenny on "Beyond the Wall."

Monterey Jazz Festival 1994

Betty Carter

She sang with swoops, soars and sass. I saw her exactly twice, each time memorable, early Monterey and later on with this shot. She was accompanied by Cyrus Chestnut on piano. He's in the picture, too.

Monterey Jazz Festival 1992

Joe Pass

Joe Pass stopped in Honolulu on his way back from Japan to play at Gabe
Baltazar's club. A couple of years before, he was in town with Oscar Peterson,
and I designed the concert poster. Before the gig at Gabe's I asked Joe if he
would autograph the poster. "You want my autograph? You haven't even heard
me play the gig yet! How do you know if I'm any good?" "Joe, I've heard you
before," I said, "Your reputation's preceded you." He was full of fun, and
great guitar.

Tech note: Kodak Safety Film 400 push to 1600, f5.6 at 1/30th of a sec.

Gabe's in Waikiki, Honolulu, Hawai'I 1980

Milt Jackson

His last note was still ringing in the air. He'd just finished his solo with Modern Jazz Quartet on "Bag's Groove," and could hear that first wave of applause from an ecstatic audience. He raised a hand as if to say, "Please, but thank you, it's okay. I do this all the time." I felt very fortunate to get this shot. Nobody else got it. I was the only one left in the pit.

Monterey Jazz Festival 1985

Stephon Harris

After Wynton called Stephon to tell him Milt Jackson died, he sat down and wrote a tune for Bags. Not too many folks knew who the young vibe player was when he took Port Townsend's stage that summer. I think he was making his first Northwest appearance. "I would like to dedicate this next tune to my mentor, Milt Jackson," Harris said. After his performance I gave Stephon my favorite print of Milt Jackson, the one on the facing page. He has this shot, too.

Centrum's Port Townsend Jazz 2000

Tal Farlow

Most guitar players don't smile when they play. But Tal Farlow was all smiles and that caught my eye at this Guitar Summit with Howard Roberts, Cal Collins, Eddie Duran, Herb Ellis and Barney Kessel. They all were having a good time, especially Farlow.

Concord Jazz Festival 1978

Ellis Larkins

Always there, steady, unruffled, dropping chords and making fills in all the right places, the piano accompanist is an unsung hero. Ellis Larkins had that ability, and he worked with the best—Ella Fitzgerald, Ruby Braff, Joe Williams, Chris Connor and Coleman Hawkins; the list goes on and on. Ellis Larkins, my choice for accompanist.

Pacific Kool Jazz Fair, Waikiki Shell, Honolulu, Hawai'i 1977

Dave Peck
& George Cables

West meets East. Seattle pianist Dave Peck and New York pianist George Cables. Two great piano players, two good friends.

Dimitriou's Jazz Alley, Seattle 2004

Kurt Elling

He swings, he scats, he's hip, he's funny, he's intellectual, he's brave, he's suave, he's eloquent; he's a poet and a crooner. He's the real deal. I could go on and on. Kurt is simply in a league of his own.

Dimitriou's Jazz Alley, Seattle 2003

Saxophone Summit

When the call came to Monterey jazz photographers for images for the 40th anniversary book, I checked proof sheets and ran across this one. You can't see everyone who's on stage, but this was some band, more like a giant jam session. Everyone had a great time, and so did I. This shot made it into that book too.

Monterey Jazz Festival 1984

The players: (l-r) George Duvivier, bass; Eddie "Lockjaw" Davis, Richie Cole, Benny Carter, Slide Hampton, Al Cohn, Carl Fontana, James Moody, Bill Berry, Eiji Kitamura, Clark Terry, Ann Patterson, and Harry "Sweets" Edison.

Sarah Vaughan

I first saw Sarah in 1959 at the second annual Monterey Jazz Festival. I was home on leave from the Air Force. No camera, just a young fan in the crowd. I was with my mom. Everybody called my mom "Tootsie"; her real name was Marie Antoinette. She was a classically trained vocalist, and she was telling me about Sarah's octave range. That's why Mom was there with me—to hear Sarah. Next time I saw her I had a camera and took this shot; she was singing "Misty." I photographed Sarah four times ('80, '81, '83 and '85) at Monterey.

Monterey Jazz Festival 1980

Pat Metheny

I took four or five rolls of Pat Metheny over a couple of decades before I got this shot. Like a lot of musical subjects, if you can't get the right angle, it doesn't work. With Pat Metheny, it seemed to work best as a straight-on shot, which I am quite pleased with. Finally.

Monterey Jazz Festival 2000

Chuck Mangione

When George Wein brought Chuck Mangione to Honolulu, I made him a poster boy. The poster featured Chuck playing flugelhorn, from a shot I took at Monterey the year before. Other artists named (but not shown) were Clark Terry, Zoot Sims, Dick Hyman, George Duvivier, and Woody Herman, and on and on. "Out of all those great players, you put me on the poster," he noted later. He was the music buzz, just hitting his stride. Of all his albums, my favorite is "Bellavia."

Pacific Kool Jazz Fair, Waikiki Shell, Honolulu, Hawai'i 1977

Billy Bang

William Walker Vincent (aka Billy Bang) studied classical violin in his youth and came under the influence of free-jazz virtuoso Leroy Jenkins, who played with Ornette Coleman and Alice Coltrane. Billy was playing hard and fast in Dizzy's Den when I walked in and what I heard made me go for this triple exposure.

Monterey Jazz Festival 2003

Tony Bennett

When I was a boy, my Dad, Oliver, owned The Hudson Music Company. The business was jukeboxes, pinball and cigarette machines. I'd hang out at the shop, sweep the floor, empty the trash—you know, kid stuff. One afternoon Columbia Records sent new 78s for the jukeboxes. "Oh, listen to this," Dad said, "This guy is terrific!" It was Tony Bennett's first release, "Because of You." Decades later after he became an icon, I was actually a little nervous photographing him for the first time. I wanted to get it right.

Tech note: Nikon F100, 180mm lens, f5.6 at 125th of a second, Kodak TMZ 3200.

Monterey Jazz Festival 2005

Count Basie

I first heard Count Basie at an outdoor roller rink on Lake Champlain in Vermont in the late '50s. Next, in Montreal on his 25th Anniversary Tour. Again in 1977. His band was the best ever that year and the next year, too. I met Count Basie once, backstage. Out of admiration, I addressed him as Mr. Basie. "Please," he said, "just call me Bill."

Monterey Jazz Festival 1977

Jon Faddis

Sunday evening, 1976 at Monterey, I first heard Jon Faddis, a 22-year-old trumpet player. Seventeen years later at the North Sea Jazz Festival at The Hague, with Seattle's Roosevelt High School jazz band, a girl in the trumpet section told me Jon Faddis was her favorite trumpet player. "Would you like to meet him?" I asked. She did—and so did Roosevelt's whole trumpet section. Jon spent the afternoon talking music to the kids. Dizzy's protege passing on the good stuff.

Monterey Jazz Festival 1976

Dizzy Gillespie

Dizzy once told me he never really cared for shots with his cheeks puffed out like balloons. He said it was too easy, a cliche. When I showed him this shot, he said, "What a job!"

Monterey Jazz Festival 1991

Shelly Manne

Just before the curtain split, while standing a few feet away I said, "Hey, Shelly, smile!" and he did. This image was taken in 1982. Two years later at Monterey, I photographed him again and he signed this photo. He died a few days later on Sept. 26, 1984, of a heart attack. He was 64. One of the most talented drummers to sit behind a drum kit.

Monterey Jazz Festival 1982

Dee Dee Bridgewater

Onstage, this is one spirited lady; she's a gifted all-around jazz performer with energy to burn. She signed this image, "Let the spirit guide you. Love, Dee Dee Bridgewater." The spirit seems to be guiding her. At the end of her encore, I wanted more. What a performer she is!

Dimitriou's Jazz Alley, Seattle 2000

Gabriel "Gabe" Baltazar Jr.

When I lived in Hawai'i, I got to know Gabe Baltazar, a veteran of 18 albums with the Stan Kenton Orchestra (1960-1965). In the early 80's, he opened his own club in Waikiki called Gabe's. I hung some of my jazz images on the walls and he booked some heavy talent: Pat Metheny, Steps Ahead, Woody Shaw and Bud Shank, to name a few. His favorite solo with Kenton was "Stairway to the Stars" which critics called "the definitive interpretation." In 2005, Gabe was named a Living Treasure of Hawai'i. I love this man. He is one of the world's great, great alto saxophone players.

Gabe's in Waikiki, Honolulu, Hawai'i 1981

Lynn Arriale

It's hard to describe this talented, beautiful lady in words but the *London Times* came close, calling her "one of the genuinely creative pianists in jazz...a superb performer...in the Bill Evans-Keith Jarrett tradition." My favorite CD is "Lynn Arriale Trio Live."

Tech note: Nikon F100, 180mm lens, f8 at 60th of a second, Kodak TMZ 32000.

Dimitriou's Jazz Alley 2005

George Benson

Early Benson—leisure suit, polka-dot shirt, great looking guitar. This is my favorite shot of George Benson. It was the first time I photographed him. He opened for Deodato, who was hot that year with "Also Sprach Zarathustra," the theme from *2001, A Space Odyssey*. George was hot, too, with his "White Rabbit" album. "Breezin'" was not to be released for another two years. I liked the shirt!

Waikiki Shell, Honolulu, Hawai'i 1974

Slide Hampton

Friday night, Monterey. Slide Hampton and the Monterey All Stars. That's what Jimmy Lyons called the lineup that included Red Holloway, Alan Dawson, Hank Jones, Mundell Lowe and Clark Terry. Funny what you noticed in a crowd. I'd seen Hampton before but never noticed he was a left-handed trombone player. Not too many of those. I lined up so that Slide's trombone was coming almost straight at me and popped this shot.

Monterey Jazz Festival 1985

Hank Jones

With a big, beautiful smile just like his two brothers' (Elvin and Thad), Hank Jones is most gracious and soft-spoken. There is fun and musical joy in this image.

Monterey Jazz Festival 1985

Ernestine Anderson

At 70-plus, Seattle's diva, Ernestine Anderson, still delivers the goods. She finished this 40-minute set fronting the Bill Ramsay Big Band with "Never Make Your Move Too Soon." And took a standing O.

Centrum's Jazz Port Townsend 2004

McCoy Tyner

Over his shoulder, through a portal from back stage with a long lens.
I would have to guess at *f*-stops. I wanted to catch motion of his hands
to show the attack, so I slowed the speed way down. I shot at 1/60 of
a second, maybe even 1/30, and as I am looking through the lens, I am
thinking, "This is the man who once played behind Billie Holiday and
Coltrane."

Monterey Jazz Festival 1991

Wallace Roney
& Wayne Shorter

The Miles Davis Tribute Band, the year after Miles died. Wallace Roney, trumpet;
Wayne Shorter, tenor and soprano saxophone; Herbie Hancock, piano; Ron Carter,
bass, and Tony Williams, drums.

Monterey Jazz Festival 1992

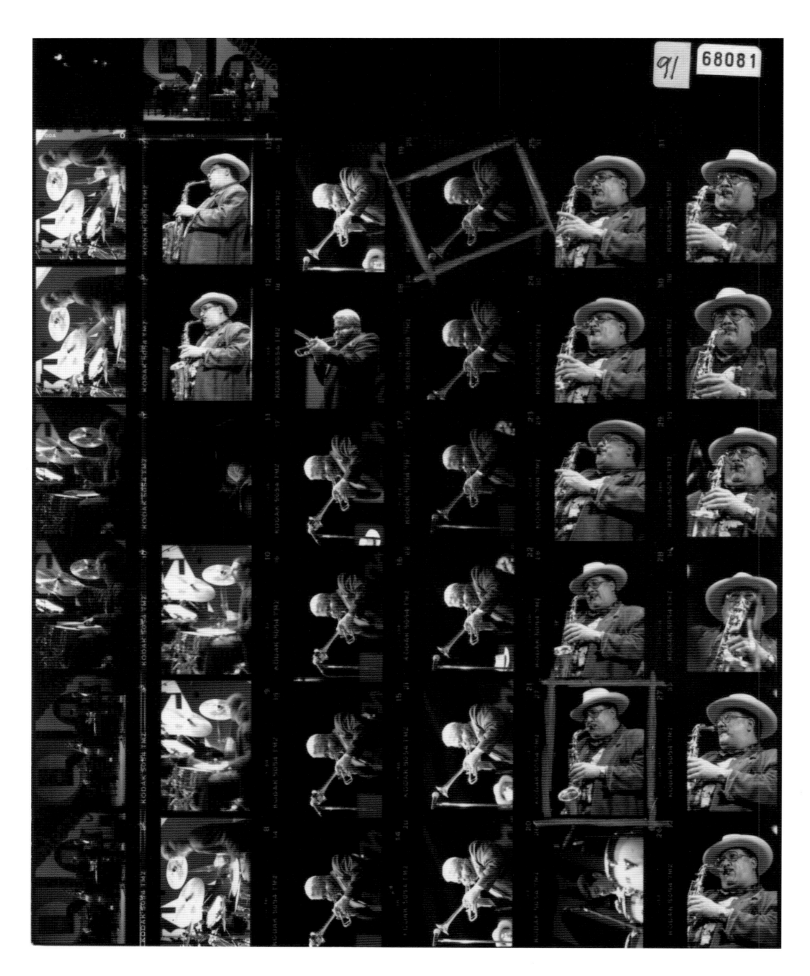

Dizzy Gillespie and Paquito D'Rivera, Monterey Jazz Festival 1991

Paquito D'Rivera

I like Paquito's hat. Sometimes I go after guys in hats, and Paquito showed up wearing this. I knew he was a good friend of Dizzy, and any friend of Dizzy is a friend of mine.

Monterey Jazz Festival 1991

George Cables

When George Cables plays "Helen's Song," an original composition, it's one of those songs that stays in your head. No matter how many times you hear it, it's like the first time. And you can't wait to hear it again.

Upstage Restaurant, Centrum's Jazz Port Townsend 2000

Brian Blade

Look at the smile on his face. I like this shot because he's doing what he loves best. He has become everyone's favorite drummer. A musician's musician.

Monterey Jazz Festival 1998

Percy Heath

A few years ago while living in Hawai'i, I got a call from New Jersey, a guy who did string instrument repair. "I handle Percy Heath's bass," he said. "Percy asked me to call you. There's a bass player magazine in the UK that's doing an article on him. Percy wants them to use the photo you gave him. Waddya say?" "If Percy liked it," I said, "let 'em use it." It's the image you see here. How could I turn down the 40-year veteran of the Modern Jazz Quartet? He gave me so much musically.

Monterey Jazz Festival 1985

Ingrid Jensen

The Nightclub at Monterey. Bad lighting conditions. One spot, little ambient light. Everybody wearing black. So I ran a whole roll of 3200 ASA, bracketed every shot, and what do you know? Out of the soup came this image. I'd rather be lucky than good.

Monterey Jazz Festival 1998

Ray Charles

Early in the set, he caught a flaw in the act, stopped the show on a dime. "Will somebody please mike that girl," Ray Charles shouted. "If you got time." The silent Ray-lette got miked, the good times rolled, again.

Monterey Jazz Festival 1987

Gerry Mulligan

For purely aesthetic reasons, I preferred photographing Gerry
Mulligan after he turned 60. His red Irish hair had turned snow
white, which made him look even more dramatic in black-and-
white photos. Especially in a tux. His playing improved too, when
he became an elder statesman. I'd followed Mulligan since the late
50s, first saw him live at Monterey and photographed him twice.
This is my favorite shot. Mulligan at 65.

Monterey Jazz Festival 1992

Dexter Gordon

The one and only time I photographed Dexter Gordon. I love the image. So much expression in his face. Look at the arched eyebrows, eyes closed. A joy to photograph. And no mistaking the Dexter Gordon sound. He said this was his best-ever touring band: George Cables, piano; Rufus Reid, bass; Eddie Gladden, drums. Bebop at its best.

Tech note: Nikon FTN, 200mm lens, f5.6 at 250th of a second, Kodak Safety Film 400 push to 1600.

Monterey Jazz Festival 1978

J. J. Johnson

J. J. Johnson and Kai Winding are the reasons why I joined the trombone club. What music the Jay and Kai Quintet made—they were a huge success, commercially and musically. "He is the definitive master of the century," trombonist Steve Turre said. "J. J. did for the trombone what Charlie Parker did for the saxophone." I photographed him twice, in 1988 and again in 1994. He died at age 77 in 2001.

Monterey Jazz Festival 1988

Ernie Andrews

Ernie Andrews, with the Central Avenue Reunion Band out of LA, sang a love song dedicated to his wife of 53 years who had just died. The song, "If I Loved You," was so beautiful I put down my camera after taking this shot and just stood there with tears in my eyes. I looked around and saw many people in the audience moved to tears, too. How he could sing that song and keep his composure was remarkable. I will never forget the moment.

Centrum's Jazz Port Townsend 1999

Bobby Shew

I'll bet you haven't seen many of these. He calls it The Shew Horn. A few years ago, I gave Bobby this photograph. "You know," he said, "I think that might have been the last time I played that horn." Whatever he plays, trumpet or flugelhorn, he's as good as it gets—a world class player, educator and clinician.

Centrum's Jazz Port Townsend 1986

Ray Brown Tribute

Have you ever seen 10 bass players on stage at one time? It was a tribute to the late Ray Brown. He was booked at Port Townsend that summer but died before the festival. John Clayton, (center) assembled this incredible collection of bass players. They played two pieces: a blues written by Ray, titled "Blues in the Basement" and a slow number with everyone playing *arco* (with bow) written by John, called "P-Ray-Lude."

Centrum's Jazz Port Townsend 2002

The players: (l-r) Clipper Anderson, Phil Baker, Anna Doak, Kristin Korb, Chuck Deardorf, John Clayton, Doug Miller, Michael Glynn, Bob Magnusson and Laura Welland

Ray Brown

I remember seeing Oscar Peterson's trio, with Ray Brown on bass and Ed Thigpen on drums, for the first time at Monterey in 1959. A banner year for me, seeing and hearing wonderful musicians who became my heroes. Ray Brown was one of them. I didn't see him again until Concord Jazz Festival in 1978, as a member of the LA Four. Got a great shot of him then, too. But everyone seems to enjoy this image most, Brown with his own trio—Benny Green, piano, and Jeff Hamilton, drums.

Monterey Jazz Festival 1994

Miles Davis

Somebody hit a sour note or wasn't on the same page. Whatever, Miles was pissed. The disapproval in his eyes is what Hawai'i folks call "stink eye." He settled down, but not much. Someone in the crowd shouted out, "Play 'Kinda Blue.'" He did—four bars, and called it a night.

Waikiki Shell, Honolulu, Hawai'i 1988

Eric Alexander

When I listen to tenor players, sometimes they all seem to have the same kind of tenor tone. I can't always tell one from the other—with the exception of Coltrane, Sonny, Getz, Dexter, Mr. "T" and this young man, who has a sound of his own. Give a listen to "Alexander the Great."

Ballard Jazz Festival, Seattle 2005

Steve Gadd

Tom Scott and the LA Express touched down in Hawai'i on the way home from Japan in 1980. From the front of the stage, I couldn't get a decent angle on Steve Gadd, so I grabbed this shot laying down on the lip of the back stage.

Tech note: Nikon FTN, 105mm lens, Ilford Safety Film 400 push to 1600.

Andrews Outdoor Amphitheatre, University of Hawai'i, Manoa, Hawai'i 1980

John Handy

When I asked John Handy to autograph this shot, he said, "Man, you made me look like a big time jazz musician!" Easy to do, because he is. He signed it: "To Ron, With Great Admiration!"

Monterey Jazz Festival 1989

Illinois Jacquet

The man from Broussard, Louisiana asked me to join his table between sets. I'd told his manager I had a couple of images I'd like to get autographed. I sat down and introduced myself. "Nice to meet you," he said. "Would you like the short name or the long one?" Honestly not knowing what he meant, I said, "I think the long one." Maybe it would be something humorous or there'd be a little drawing of a saxophone. I didn't know. It turned out to be his full name: "Jean-Baptiste Illinois Jacquet."

Monterey Jazz Festival 1989

Joe La Barbara

Joe La Barbara came into my consciousness in the mid-70's when he was keeping time for Chuck Mangione, Bill Evans, and then Tony Bennett. I didn't meet him until a few years ago, doing a photo shoot for pianist Dave Peck. Joe was part of the trio with bassist Jeff Johnson. I'm crazy about his brush work, reminiscent of Shelly Manne.

Centrum's Jazz Port Townsend 2003

Mark Murphy

I believe the world has only a handful of real jazz singers, and Mark Murphy is one of them. Asked by *Down Beat Magazine* how he became a jazz singer, he answered for all jazz singers: "We were chosen. We didn't choose it. They came and said, 'You are a bebop baby.' We're prisoners of love." I first heard him in 1979, on a little radio station in Hawai'i that played an hour or two of jazz, programmed by my friend Michael Bloom. I ran out and bought Murphy's latest release at the time, "Satisfaction Guaranteed."

Centrum's Jazz Port Townsend 1986

Thad Jones

From the jazz family of Hank and Elvin Jones, middle brother Thad was a self-taught trumpet player with the Count Basie Band. An arranger and composer who wrote the haunting standard, "A Child Is Born," he and drummer Mel Lewis formed the Thad Jones/Mel Lewis Big Band in '65, and won a Grammy Award for "Live In Munich." He moved to Denmark to teach at the Royal Danish Conservatory. He died in 1986.

Monterey Jazz Festival 1978

Michel Petrucciani

I first heard and photographed Michel Petrucciani in Honolulu at the Pacific Ballroom of the Ilikai Hotel in 1983. I remember it well because I designed the poster for promoter Tom Moffatt, a jazz junkie like me. The bill was the Charles Lloyd Quartet, featuring Michel. I knew who Charles was, but had no idea about Michel. What a pleasant surprise! What a huge talent.

Monterey Jazz Festival 1990

Max Roach

All drummers are my heroes. Especially Max Roach. In Atlanta in 1997, he did a 45-minute set with his drum kit, nothing else, no one else. Amazing. Under a single spot, at 73, he delivered a primal beat, totally improv, steady hand, tight focus, clear direction: The man in his moment. "Take all the pictures you want," his road manager said. He knew too.

Atlanta Jazz Festival 1997

Pharoah Sanders

Sanders was born Farrell Sanders, but Sun Ra called him "Pharoah" and it stuck (Sun Ra was born Herman Poole Blount). Sanders started playing tenor in Oakland and came to prominence in 1965 with John Coltrane, recording seven albums with him, including "Ascension" and "Meditations." In 2006 he played jazz's hallowed ground, Grace Cathedral in San Francisco. Listen to his 2003 recording, "The Creator Has A Master Plan."

Atlanta Jazz Festival 1997

Dave Brubeck
& Donald Johanos

Dave and Donald. Take Five meets the Maestro at rehearsal in Honolulu
Concert Hall. It only took a few minutes. Brubeck and Johanos met, talked
charts, ran through a couple of tunes, made up the play list, said *aloha*. I
couldn't have staged this shot better.

Honolulu Concert Hall 1981, Hawai'i

Buddy Rich

Backstage, before the curtain, who knows about Buddy? Some days he's Mr. Nice. Next day he might fire his whole trumpet section. This night, he was playful. He saw me shooting and tipped his cymbal toward the kleig lights, trying to overexpose the image. I fixed him in the lab for a fun shot.

Monterey Jazz Festival 1979

Carmen McRae

It was a special Silver Anniversary concert on Thursday night before the 25th Annual Monterey Jazz Festival began. This was the only time I photographed Carmen McRae. She closed the "Gala Showcase Concert" that night, but not before I ran a roll and got this shot.

Tech note: Nikon FM2, 105mm lens, Kodak Safety Film 400 push to 1600.

Monterey Jazz Festival 1982

Alex Acuna

If you hit, shake, or rattle it, you're a percussionist. Peruvian-born Alex
Acuna is at home with a rack of percussion instruments. He played in local
bands as a boy, joined the Perez Prado band, played Vegas in 1974 with Elvis
and Diana Ross, then joined the jazz fusion group, Weather Report and recorded "Black Market" and "Heavy Weather." He toured and recorded with
Herbie Hancock, Dave Grusin, Carlos Santana, Wayne Shorter, Joni Mitchell
and Al Jarreau, and taught at UCLA and Berklee College of Music in Boston.

Monterey Jazz Festival 2000

Jeff Hamilton

Several years ago at Centrum's Jazz Port Townsend, Jeff was playing the festival and doing the drum clinics. I had a photo of him I'd taken at the Concord Jazz Festival when he was with the LA Four. As we talked I said that I played the drums too, but I'm really a part-timer. I asked him to autograph the photo, and he did. "To Ron, from one part-timer to another, Best Wishes—Jeff Hamilton."

Tech note: Nikon F100, 80mm lens, f5.6 at 60th of a second, Kodak TMZ 3200.

Monterey Jazz Festival 2003

Jimmy Heath

In 1976 Jimmy Heath premiered The *Afro-American Suite of Evolution* at Monterey with 13 suites including African Percussion, Field Holler, Ragtime, Blues, Swing, and ending with Avant Garde. A large production, it included the Monterey Jazz Festival All-Star Band with Jimmy's two brothers, Percy on bass, Albert "Tootie" Heath on drums. Years later the Heath brothers were in Seattle. And I was lucky to find once again all three brothers in the same place at the same time. I had all three sign prints for me, and they each got one, too.

Monterey Jazz Festival 1985

Joshua Redman

Joshua Redman often keeps time by hopping from one foot to the next.
Noticed that the first time I saw him and couldn't resist the shot.

Monterey Jazz Festival 1998

Nnenna Freelon

When I shoot I try for angles in an image. This image of Nnenna is a good example. Both arms are parallel angles, framing her face, so no matter where you look you always come back to her face, so expressive. Got lucky again here. Monterey had a new rule for shooters that year: two tunes and out. This was my first shot.

Tech note: Nikon 8008s, 180mm lens, f5.6 at 125th of a second, Kodak TMZ 2300.

Monterey Jazz Festival 2003

Branford Marsalis

Two-time Grammy winner Branford Marsalis, eldest of the Marsalis brothers, is perhaps the most innovative. He worked in Art Blakey's Big Band and the Jazz Messengers, joined brother Wynton's group, set up his own group, and from 1992 to 1995, was the Tonight Show's musical director. In the early '90's he appeared with the Grateful Dead and toured with Miles Davis.

Monterey Jazz Festival 2001

Freddie Green

I was fortunate to see and hear Freddie Green live with the Count Basie Band several times. After Freddie joined the band in 1937, it was called the All American Rhythm Section—Basie on piano, Walter Page on bass, Jo Jones on drums, and Freddie on guitar. The four had a sense of unity and rhythmic flow like no other. He stayed with Basie 50 years, longer than any other musician. Freddie pioneered the way guitar is played in a big band setting. He was smooth and accurate.

Monterey Jazz Festival 1976

Anita O'Day

If you want to see this lady in performance, pick up "Jazz On A Summer's Day," a DVD of the 1958 Newport Jazz Festival. She's on stage with a big, white wide-brimmed summer hat, in a polka dot dress, singing, "Tea for Two." I only saw her once; this photo is it. She died on Thanksgiving Day, 2006.

Gabe's in Waikiki, Honolulu, Hawai'i 1980

Dee Dee Rainbow

A fixture at Monterey, Dee Dee Rainbow (that's her real name) is a retired Seattle art teacher who absolutely loves and celebrates jazz in her own colorful way. Here, late on Sunday night, dressed in her rainbow best, with the festival winding down, she makes her exit stage left. It's all over now but the memories.

Tech note: Nikon 8008s, 35mm lens, f5.6 at 60th of a second, Kodak TMZ 3200.

Monterey Jazz Festival 1999

Acknowledgments

Rick Carroll and Marcie Carroll for your words, encouragement and tenacity to bring a long-ago vision to reality.

Dr. Herb Wong, thank you for the insightful thoughts in your intro. What a maestro! And, of course, your friendship over the years.

Hank Curaza, the inspiration for it all.

Photographers Robert Knight, Bob DeMello, Ric Noyle, Carl Shaneff, Ray Avery, Elde Stewart, and my Dad, Oliver. You all gave me the gift of your photographic knowledge.

Tom Moffatt and Gabe Baltazar for bringing jazz where there was none. John Leonard for the credential letter.

Ernie Beyl and Paul Fingerote for all the Monterey press assistance.

Richard Soden, my dear, late friend; for 22 years, every third weekend in September I had a fun place to stay.

Jim Wilson and Berit Keeble, Tedd and Kathy Kraft, for your friendship and Carmel Valley hospitality.

My MJF box-mates Jimmy and Marie Lofton, for camaraderie and friendship.

Special thanks to John Dimitriou for allowing an ongoing exhibit of my work at Jazz Alley over the years.

John Clayton, Chuck Deardorf and Michael Bloom for remembering what I forgot. Rob Perry, for the good seat, right down front.

Michael Ricci and Jason West, All About Jazz, thank you. Rachael Millikan for all your help. Fausto Torres, for the great lighting on the Jazz Alley stage.

Scott Brown, for the Montreux and North Sea jazz festivals.

Jim Wilke, for meticulous record keeping and keeping the flame alive.

Doug Ramsey, for the review. Kate Bourne, for a great story. Kurt Elling, for your encouragement.

Keven Elliff at Centrum Arts and Dennis Haskell for making the exhibits easy.

Beki McMillan at Eastern Offset Printing Co. in Atlantic Beach, NC, for layout and design of this book.

John Bishop, Matt Jorgensen, for all the fun at the Ballard Jazz Festival and in New York.

Bailey, JoAnn and Teri, my siblings, thank you for your support.

My daughters and families, Lynn and Randy "Big Guy" Levinson, Chloe Belle Levinson, Rhonda and Raymond Key, Jennifer Waters and Joe Harrill.

Bellevue Art and Frame for help with exhibits.

Mark Schneider, my webmaster.

Panda Lab staff for help in everything black-and-white.

Bob Hatch at Mercer Island Lab.

Sandy Seigle, for loving my work.

Dr. Harry Shriver at GHC for keeping me healthy.

Brian Blevins, for help in the early days.

Diana Higgins and Laurent Davidson for Carmel hospitality.

And, finally, thank you to all the wonderful and talented musicians who helped make this dream come true.

Sources:

Books

Ian Carr, Digby Fairweather & Brian Priestly, *Jazz: The Rough Guide The Essential Companion to Artists & Albums*, Viking/Penguin, 1995/2000.

William Claxton, *Jazz*, Chronicle Books, 1996

Richard Cook & Brian Morton, *The Penguin Guide to Jazz on CD, LP & Cassette*, (7th Edition) Penguin Books, 2004

Leonard Feather & Ira Gitler, *The Biographical Encyclopedia of Jazz*, Oxford University Press, USA; Rev Ed edition (November 18, 1999)

John Fordham, *Jazz*, Music Sales Corp., (1st American edition) 1993.

Dizzy Gillespie, *To Bop or Not to Bop Memoirs of Dizzy Gillespie*, Doubleday Books, (1st edition) 1979.

Jimmy Lyons & Ira Kamin, *Dizzy, Duke, The Count and Me*, The Story of the Monterey Jazz Festival, A California Living Book, San Francisco Examiner Division of The Hearst Corp., 1978

William Minor & Bill Wishner, *Monterey Jazz Festival, Forty Legendary Years*, Angel City Press, Santa Monica, 1997.

William Minor, *Jazz Journeys to Japan*, University of Michigan Press, 2004.

Doug Ramsey, *The Private and Public Lives of Paul Desmond*, Parkside Publications, Inc., Seattle 2005

Ken Burns & Geoffrey C. Ward, *Jazz A History of America's Music*, Alfred A. Knopf, New York 2000.

Newspapers

Various profiles, reviews, articles and obituaries which have appeared over past 40 years in *The New York Times, San Francisco Chronicle, Monterey Herald, Los Angeles Times, Seattle Times, Honolulu Advertiser and Honolulu Star-Bulletin.*

Websites

www.allaboutjazz.com
www.allmusicguide.com/
www.answers.com
www.bobbyshew.com/
www.cleolaine.com/
www.internationaljazzproductions.com/
www.iaje.org/
www.joelocke.com/
www.kurtelling.com/
www.tierneysutton.com/
www.quarternotes.com/
en.wikipedia.org/wiki/Main_Page

Ron Hudson

Born in Oakland, California, he grew up surrounded by jazz in his father's music shop and became a young jazz fan in the '50s. A graphic artist in New York, California and Hawai'i, he played drums on weekends. In the 1970s, he began photographing jazz artists in night clubs, concerts and festivals, documenting jazz history.

Sandy Seigle Photo

He has photographed more than 900 jazz artists, covered festivals from Montreux to Monterey. His images appear on CD covers, magazines, art exhibits, private collections of many jazz artists, and are part of an everchanging exhibit in Seattle at Dimitriou's Jazz Alley.

He is a member of the International Association for Jazz Education.

He lives in Seattle with his wife, Christine, and miniature poodle Ella Fitz.

Index